The Resilient Runner:

Mental Toughness Training for
Endurance Runners

by William A. Peters

Copyright © William A. Peters
(2014). All rights reserved.

Table of Contents

THE RESILIENT RUNNER

Foreword

I became interested in sports psychology relatively late in my amateur athletic career. This is unfortunate for me because knowing the fundamentals of mental toughness would have made me a much better endurance runner in my youth. For runners to reach their potential, they require not only a high level of physical fitness but also an equally high level of mental fitness. Elite runners are extraordinary individuals, not purely because of their athletic abilities, but also because of their extraordinary psychology. Olympic teams travel with their own sports psychologist who helps the athletes handle anxiety, negative thoughts, self-doubt, pre-race jitters and other psychological barriers to success. Even amateur coaches want their runners to be mentally tough. However, most amateur runners don't know about mental conditioning, and most amateur coaches don't create a mental conditioning program for their runners. The runner is often left with such well-worn aphorisms as "Well, you have to develop the proper mental attitudes" or "You have to be confident and possess the will to win." But how does one "be confident" or "develop the proper mental attitudes?" These questions are usually left unanswered. The good news is that I learned through over twenty-five years of endurance running that you do not have to be born with mental toughness. Mental toughness is an acquired trait. You don't have to go through a life-threatening experience to gain it. I don't guarantee that you'll win your next race after reading this book, but I do guarantee that you will become a mentally tougher runner and will likely beat your P.R. (personal record) if you learn the techniques in this book. This is the book I wish I'd been given when I was a young runner.

I began endurance running in elementary school. The cross country coach of our school had me and my teammates run laps of our school's asphalt parking lot in the noonday heat--one way to develop mental toughness! One important lesson I've learned over decades of running since then is that runners focus too much on the physical side of our sport: leg length, weight, VO2 max, arm carriage, stride frequency, heart rate, lactate threshold, running economy and other factors. These might contribute to you setting a P.R. and even to better health, but they don't define you as a runner. The gray matter between your ears is far more important to your success than your muscle fiber. If you want to succeed as a lifelong runner, you'll gain more payback from brain training than from physical training.

Many good books exist on how to train your body so that you can become a better runner, as do many good general books on sports psychology. But there are very few good books on mental toughness training for runners. This is strange because, of all athletes, endurance runners most need mental toughness to succeed. My disappointment with the lack of good books on the psychological aspects of running led me to write this book. My goal is to help you become better aware of the psychological skills you possess and to teach you techniques to strengthen your mental toughness. This book will teach you, among other lessons, the psychological skills that are necessary to set proper goals, build your confidence, rebound from setbacks, and visualize yourself to success in endurance running. The book is designed to help you become focused so that you avoid negative thoughts during competitions. It also seeks to help you derive more enjoyment from running. In short, reading this book and following my advice will help you to become the best runner you can be.

CHAPTER ONE

Qualities of Successful Endurance Runners

"If there's one thing we runners do, it's endure. We endure through long runs and hard workouts, weeks of bad weather, and days of low energy. We do what it takes to see things through to the end." - Scott Douglas

"Mind is everything. Muscle—just pieces of rubber. All that I am, I am because of my mind." - Paavo Nurmi

Certain characteristics set elite runners apart from other runners and contribute to their overall success. These characteristics are both physiological and psychological. You can improve your performance by modeling your psychological behavior on that of elite runners. Below are some of the psychological characteristics that set elite runners apart from the pack.

Motivated

Motivation is high on the list of successful

runners' primary qualities. Runners must be highly motivated in order to maintain their focus on their running goals. This motivation must come from within the runner rather than through the influence of others. This high level of motivation ensures that elites maintain their training programs over the long term and ultimately see success.

Positive Outlook

Elite runners are able to identify self-defeating thoughts and challenge them with encouraging statements. When a negative thought strikes, they stop it in its tracks.

Focused

Elite runners are able to focus in the face of distractions or unexpected circumstances. The mentally tough runner doesn't avoid challenging situations, but instead addresses them right away. One could describe this as a sort of introversion or self-centeredness. It allows the runner to give single-minded attention to the task of running and to the state of her body as she pursues the task at hand. Because of this ability to focus, successful runners have a heightened sense of awareness that allows them to "listen" closely to their bodies: they are able to manage their energy reserves well, to pace themselves, and to sense when it is right to hold back and when to shift into a higher gear.

Resilient

Successful runners are able to bounce back from adversity, pain or a disappointing performance. The mentally tough runner can realize and admit a mistake, understand a missed opportunity, isolate the lesson, and quickly move on to focus on the immediate goal ahead. Mental toughness is built by doing difficult tasks over and over again, especially when you don't feel like doing them. Our society has conditioned us to believe that there should be no discomfort, to stop when we are uncomfortable. But the discomfort we feel when we're doing a challenging workout is an important part of the strengthening process. It's important to push through your down days when you're not feeling your best. Dogged determination requires keeping your feet moving forward through inconveniences, discomfort, insecurities, and pain to reach your goals.

Confident

Confidence is a crucial trait. Highly confident runners can anticipate success and work towards achieving it. They also trust their capabilities. Because they are optimistic, they are not scared of trying new things. They may fail, but they will get up again because they know they have it in them to win. An elite runner's confidence is realistic.

Able to channel anxiety productively

It is important for runners to be able to feel anxiety. Anxiety helps the runner to recognize the competition's talent, to accurately assess it and strive to defeat it. By contrast, runners who feel anxious but don't have the capacity to channel this anxiety into the development of their competitive capacity fare badly. Ultimately, elite runners are distinguished by their capacity to deal effectively with their anxiety by channeling it into productive activity.

Able to Visualize Results

Elite runners see an objective, even when there are no immediate signs of getting closer to it. The mentally tough runner creates a clear picture of the goal, visualizes it often, and keeps that image in the forefront of his mind no matter the circumstances. Elite runners imagine all the possible scenarios that might arise in a race, and have a plan for moving through each one successfully.

The following chapters explain techniques that can be used to develop these qualities.

CHAPTER TWO

The Nature of Motivation

"Running every day is a kind of lifeline for me, so I'm not going to lay off or quit just because I'm busy. If I used being busy as an excuse not to run, I'd never run again. I have only a few reasons to keep on running, and a truckload of them to quit. All I can do is keep those few reasons nicely polished." - Haruki Murakami

"Motivation is what gets you started. Habit is what keeps you going."- Jim Ryun

In many endeavors, motivation has been institutionalized. We study hard in school because teachers and parents encourage us to. We work hard in business to please managers. Running, however, is usually a personal activity, and is often lonely. Runners, then, must motivate themselves. Unfortunately, most people misunderstand motivation. They wait until they are motivated to do something, which results in procrastination. If you wait until you feel motivated before you start running, you may have to wait forever.

Motivation works like this:

A small action creates motivation which leads to more action.

Motivation is often spoken of as if it was contained in some inward reservoir. Whether it's talking about one's level of motivation, waiting for motivation, or digging deep to find motivation, motivation is frequently discussed as a quantity. But you are likely to be troubled by too many motivations: the motivation to sit, the motivation to watch T.V., the motivation to eat, the motivation to live a long and healthy life, and others. You constantly sort and re-sort your motivations. All of your pressures, wants, and needs are being re-sorted by daily and hourly reminders. Which motivation makes it to the top of the heap is determined by a combination of needs, internal states, external reminders, memories, and roadblocks. As such, a reliance on feelings of motivation is a recipe for failure. You need to create self-reinforcing, motivational patterns that build a strong foundation that bolsters your running. Running is easy: Put one foot in front of the other. Staying motivated to run is challenging. It takes thinking and planning. It takes believing in yourself and the value of your running. It takes a powerful web of attitudes and practices that make your daily exercise as regular as brushing your teeth. In short, you need to learn strategies for manipulating your feelings of motivation.

The following chapters contain strategies on how to prime the motivation pump.

CHAPTER THREE

Become an Intrinsic Runner

"The human body is capable of amazing physical deeds. If we could just free ourselves from our perceived limitations and tap into our internal fire, the possibilities are endless." – Dean Karnazes

"Running is all about having the desire to train and persevere until every fiber in your legs, mind, and heart is turned to steel. And when you're finally forged hard enough, you will become the best runner you can be. And that's all that you can ask for." – Paul Maurer

We runners are acutely aware of our performances over time. In many other sports, participants are less aware of their declining abilities. Significant numbers of runners stop running in their late 20s when they realize their race times are no longer improving. Participant numbers thin dramatically in the 60s and beyond. By stopping, these runners fail to gain the health benefits that running provides over a lifetime.

THE RESILIENT RUNNER

You won't adhere to any running program without having inner reasons for doing so. The technical training in other running books is important, but changing your mindset is far more important than any technical training. All the technical training books in the world are useless if you can't get yourself to run regularly. Runners who successfully maintain a running regimen learn to shift their focus from distant, external outcomes such as losing weight to positive, internal experiences in the present. They transform their thoughts and feelings to make running an enjoyable and uplifting experience. They become "intrinsic runners." The philosophy of intrinsic running is based on years of scientific research. A seminal paper on intrinsic motivation by Robert White, Ph.D. was published in the Psychological Review in 1959. Other parts of the theory are derived from the work of Mihaly Csikszentmihalyi (pronounced "MEE-hy CHEEK-sent-mə-HY-ee"), Ph.D., on the concept of flow. Numerous studies on motivation and physical activity have been published since. Stated simply, intrinsic motivation is motivation that comes from within. Intrinsically motivated individuals engage in activities that interest them, and they engage in them freely, with a full sense of personal control. There is no sense of engaging in an activity for a material reward. Intrinsic motivation is little more than taking part in an interesting activity simply because of love for the activity.

The core concept behind intrinsic running is to run for its own sake. If you don't get something out of each run, you're likely to cease running. You will need to achieve three specific mental states to develop a mindset powerful enough to motivate you to run-- and like it--under any conditions. They are: personal meaning, mastery, and flow.

Personal meaning orientation helps you to find running rewarding in and of itself. You use running to explore who you are. Intrinsic runners articulate why they are running and what they hope to get from it. Ask yourself, "What do I need to do to feel I have accomplished something meaningful and challenging?" Write down your answers in your running journal (see the following chapters on journaling and goal-setting for more details). Only when running becomes personally meaningful will you be motivated to do it regularly.

Next, you must learn to monitor improvements in your performance, a concept known as mastery. We habitually attempt to master our surroundings, and when we're successful we feel pleasure. In the case of mastery orientation, the goal is mastery of running. Perceived ability for the mastery-oriented individual is a function of perceived improvement from one point in time to the next. The task-oriented athlete perceives herself to be of high ability if she can perform a task better today than she could in the past. The mastery-oriented individual continues to work for mastery of running, and enjoys feelings of self-efficacy and confidence in so doing. Runners with a mastery orientation derive a sense of achievement from successful task completion such as skill improvement, performing at one's best, or demonstrating competence. Competence motivation can be increased if you feel good about your running regardless of the outcome. Effort and improvement should be emphasized rather than--or at least in addition to--winning races. Intrinsic runners focus on challenging themselves and meeting personal goals, such as setting a P.R., instead of comparing themselves to other runners, which can be frustrating and intimidating. Statements that represent mastery orientation include "I ran to the best of my ability" and "I beat my P.R." A mastery focus helps keep you motivated. Mastery-oriented runners drop out of running less often than do those who whose satisfaction from running is more dependent on event outcomes.

Perhaps the best way to stay intrinsically motivated during exercise is to reach "flow," an optimal psychological state involving total absorption in an activity. Flow is an energized mental state that occurs when a person is totally focused on, and immersed in, an activity and the challenge matches a person's level of skill. Flow is all about staying in the moment. Being *"in the zone"* is another way of describing flow. An example of flow is Roger Bannister's description of his breaking the four-minute mile barrier, "No longer conscious of my movement, I discovered a new unity with nature. I had found a new source of power and beauty, a source I never dreamt existed."

The father of flow Mihaly Csikszentmihalyi first defined flow in his 1975 book *Beyond Boredom and*

Anxiety: Experiencing Flow in Work and Play. Csikszentmihalyi found that this state is most likely to occur in a person when the level of the challenge a person undertakes is matched to his skill level. In a 1992 study, Susan Jackson, Ph.D. interviewed 28 elite athletes across seven sports and found that the key factors contributing to flow are confidence, focus, how the performance felt and progressed, and motivation and arousal levels. She also found that athletes perceived the flow state within their control. According to 1999 studies by Jackson and Csikszentmihalyi, the relationship between an athlete's confidence and the challenge being faced is the main factor in determining whether an athlete experiences competitive flow. He outlined several strategies for finding flow in physical activity. Here are some:

- Set clear goals. With flow, it's not achieving an endpoint that's important; it's the process of achieving. But without clear, specific goals, it is difficult to concentrate on your actions and avoid distractions.
- Tune in to feedback. Learn to gauge feedback that the mind and body provide during exercise. Staying aware of your progress during your workout keeps you connected to what your body is doing and how it's feeling.
- Balance perceived challenge and skill. You must create new challenges for yourself, setting goals that make you work harder. But keep in mind, though, that when challenging yourself beyond your skill level, you may

become frustrated and avoid running. Adjust by setting more realistic goals.

The key to achieving flow is to practice a skill to the point where it becomes so ingrained in your brain that you don't have to think about what you're doing. If you can reach a state of flow, you'll want to run again and again to attain that positive state of mind. The trick to staying in the flow state is to continually increase the challenge as your skills improve.

In order to run regularly for the rest of your life, you must work from the inside out. As you begin to run for the inner rewards of the activity itself, you will find yourself going for a run not because you have to, but because you want to.

CHAPTER FOUR

Journaling

"I keep a training journal, where I write down all my workouts: split times, heart rates, and how I felt that day. It gives me a sense of accomplishment to see the workout written down on paper, and it also allows me to track my progress. There's nothing more motivating than seeing steady improvements. And, when I don't improve, it helps me to have a record so I can figure out why." – Caryn Parmentier Davies

"The night before the race and a couple nights before I look through my log book. I look through great workouts I've had and I look at workouts that weren't so great but that I still completed and got the most out of it that I could. That just helps me realize that there's going to be ups and downs in every training block and in every race. You just have to kind of stick with it and remind yourself you've been there and fought through it before and you can do it again." – Kara Goucher

"It's a fact that those who journal their running tend to run more days per year." -Jeff Galloway

One mistake I made when I began running was not keeping a running journal. I ran for years before I started keeping a journal. Had I kept a journal from the start of my running, my progress would have accelerated. Organization is what separates the runner from the jogger. Runners make more progress because they schedule for their success, and to avoid injuries, while joggers just get out there when they can. The running journal (also known as a training log) is a runner's tradition that has been around for many decades. It goes back at least as far as Alfred Shrubb, a legendary English runner born in 1878 who kept detailed notes about his runs. This impulse to keep a running journal is a natural one for runners. Running 20, 30, 40 or more kilometers per week, month after month, is a significant achievement, but unlike other concrete achievements, we can't see and touch our running achievements. By keeping a training journal, we make our running achievements visible. Pride is only one reason for keeping a journal, though; other reasons are detailed in the following.

Why Keep a Running Journal?

Training Analysis and Troubleshooting

A running journal helps you determine how well your training is going. It does so by enabling you to connect cause and effect. By reviewing your running journal, you can determine whether you need to run more kilometers or less, whether you need to do more speedwork, and so on. There is always a more effective way to train. Keeping a journal makes that more effective method easier to find. Things inevitably go wrong during training. You get injured, plateau, and have bad races. Figuring out the cause of each setback will help you to avoid future setbacks. Your journal contains the information you need to troubleshoot your problems. Your journal also helps you to see patterns in training and racing that reveal optimal methods and strategies. By reading over your journal on a regular basis, you may find that certain workouts made you feel fit and confident, leading to your best performances.

Motivation and Accountability

Training can be a grind through which it's difficult to stay motivated. Your training journal can help you avoid drops in motivation by reinforcing your investment in your goals. Your journal can be a great source of motivation because it shows all the hard work you've completed and the progress you've made. When you review your journal, you'll likely think something similar to "I can't stop now. Look at how much work I've done!" For more inspiration and guidance, you can fill your journal with quotes and tips from running magazines and books such as this one.

Journaling helps you monitor improvements in your performance, a concept known as mastery. A mastery focus keeps you motivated. If you really want to run regularly for the rest of your life, you need to run for the inner rewards of the activity itself.

Confidence Building

The runners who most often achieve their goals are the confident ones. Your training log can be a great source of confidence. It's a rich record of how much progress you've made. It's inspiring to look back at the challenging workouts you have conquered. Your log is the nearest thing you have to proof that you can achieve your goals before you actually achieve them.

Self-Knowledge

Each runner is unique. Therefore, no two runners can get their best results by training in exactly the same way. One of your most important duties as a runner is to learn about your running self so that you can use this self-knowledge to refine your training. Your journal provides a wealth of information through which to develop such self-knowledge.

Experimentation and Dreaming

A running journal allows you to experiment and dream. During your running career, you will likely encounter new training ideas that you'll want to try. Your running journal is the best place in which to record your experimentation with each new training idea. It provides an objectivity that doesn't exist in casual trials of ideas. Behave like a sports scientist: introduce one change to your training at a time and look at the results. Have your times for certain distances/routes decreased? Do you feel better during or after runs? Is your recovery period shorter? Journals are the perfect place in which to record visions (optimistic but realistic projections of what you think you can attain 6 or 12 months ahead) and to construct a training plan to transform those visions into accomplishable goals.

What Should I Record?

Your journal can be as simple or as complicated as you want it to be. Many runners start by recording their run times and distances on a wall calendar. I started journaling by recording run times and distances, and morning heart rate in a loose-leaf folder. I recommend that you start by recording in an inexpensive notebook a few selections from this list :

- Time of your run
- Distance
- Morning heart rate, to judge general fatigue level
- How you felt ("Great", "Alright", "Sluggish", etc.)
- Weather conditions (temperature, humidity, wind speed, etc.)
- Time of the day, as it may influence how you feel
- Terrain, as certain terrain may cause injuries
- Your body weight, if your are trying to lose weight
- Your diet

- Aches and pains. Noting sore spots helps you identify causes of injuries
- Shoes, in order to track usage and replace on a sensible schedule
- Sleep, since it affects running performance
- A daily or weekly goal, so that each run has a purpose
- Split times from speed sessions, to gauge training progress
- Walk breaks, as they indicate how you were feeling
- Thoughts, especially negative ones, during runs

Start listening to yourself during runs. What you do in training you likely also will do in racing (such as being tough or caving in). Pay close attention to your self-talk, how you think and run and meet your workout goals. Did a positive thought result in stronger running? Did a negative thought result in a weaker effort? Record all of this as soon as you can in your journal. Do it for every run, even easy ones. Soon, a pattern will reveal itself. You'll find out how negative you've been, and exactly what thoughts may have been standing in the way of reaching your potential (for more details see Chapter 8: How to Talk to Yourself About Running).

Later, you can switch to a more sophisticated option such as a specialized running journal, smart phone app, or Website. Specialized running journals have information and inspiration, while software products such as apps and Websites allow you to set up a training program, and to collect, sort, and analyze data efficiently to track your progress. The software products make it easier to record data by asking you to fill in the blanks. Several software products allow you to sort through months or years to look for trends, causes of injuries, or reasons for success. I currently use a smartphone app that is linked with a Website. I bring my smartphone for the first few runs of a new route and use the app to automatically track the details of the run. Thereafter, I use my digital watch to record my run time for those runs, and manually enter the details of a run on the Website. Whatever option you choose, your running will improve by logging your runs in a journal.

CHAPTER FIVE

Goal Setting

"The trick is striving for the goal, but being grateful for the progress if you don't happen to reach it. If I fall short, I still have the strength and training behind me as I set out for my next goal. I set myself up the best I can to achieve a race goal. When I fall short, there is always something to be grateful for and it's usually that I became stronger and healthier in the process." - Deena Kastor

"I knew going into each race that my confidence would help to support a fast day and a successful outcome. After transitioning from coaching myself to coaching others, I knew the best place to start was to establish and build upon an athlete's confidence level. The technical stuff is secondary if you don't have the inner-drive, mental edge and physical foundation to take the leap." - Dave Scott

"You have to wonder at times what you're doing out there. Over the years, I've given myself a thousand reasons to keep running, but it always comes back to where it started. It comes down to self-

*satisfaction and a sense of achievement." - Steve
Prefontaine*

Goal setting gives focus and purpose to training, which in turn creates motivation. Having goals and reasons for pursuing them will help get you out running on low-motivation days, will help keep you going when the obstacles are daunting, will lead to your greatest achievements, and will ensure that you fully savor the joy of those achievements.

Why Does Goal Setting Work?

Goal setting is often advocated as a means to improve performance in running, but you rarely hear explanations of why it works. Goal setting improves performance by directing attention, increasing effort and persistence, and motivating the runner to develop new learning strategies. When a runner does not have a goal, her attention wanders from one thought to another without any particular direction. Setting a specific goal causes the runner to focus her attention on this goal and upon the tasks associated with it. Once a runner's attention is directed toward a particular goal, she increases her effort during training to accomplish the goal. Most runners can focus their attention and effort on improving for an entire training session, but to be successful, a runner must persist for a long time. Persistence is a by-product of effective goal setting. As long as the goal is present and the athlete wants to obtain it, she will persist in the effort needed to accomplish it. Goal-setting also promotes the development of new learning strategies. Without goals for improvement, a runner is content to get along with the learning strategies and skills that she currently possesses. The setting of new goals leads the runner to learn more about running.

When you set goals they should be:

Specific and measurable. They should be clear, direct, and objective. For example, "My goal is to run this year's marathon in less than 3 hours."

Within a time frame. "My goal is to run a 5K in 18:00 by this June." Without a time frame, there is really nothing to challenge you to attain your goal because you can keep putting it off.

Positive. Positive goals create a positive state of mind. "My goal is to finish in the top 500 of the marathon" is better than "I don't want to finish behind 500 in the marathon."

Challenging. They should not be easy.

Realistic. They should not be out of your reach.

Recorded. In your running journal, of course.

Goal setting is only helpful if the goals you set for yourself are actually the right ones in the first place. Your goals must be realistic. Otherwise, the very targets that are supposed to be motivating you will end up discouraging you. Many self-help writers encourage people to set stretch goals; that is, to "reach for the stars", but this is bad advice if the stars are not within reach. People only achieve stretch goals 10% of the time, and successively failing to achieve goals creates a downward spiral in which performance becomes ever more impaired as motivation and confidence decline. Confidence is critical. Confidence comes from hard evidence of what you can do; how fast you have proved to your brain that you can go in training. You should approach training as a means of building confidence in your ability to achieve your race goals. Create short term goals that are designed to maximize your confidence. Set yourself up for success in training. Do everything you can to minimize the number of failures you experience in training. Don't fret about the technical details of training. Think about the training goals you need to reach in order to arrive on the starting line feeling confident in your ability to achieve your race goals. The point of training is to get ready to achieve race goals, and the best indicator of readiness to achieve race goals is confidence. This is something that elite runners know, but amateur runners miss.

To create your goals, consider the question: What do I want to accomplish in running? Think about 3 time frames: career, medium-term (1-2 years into the future), and short-term (6 months into the future). Running goals typically include such hallmarks as placing high within your age group, achieving a personal best, qualifying for a particular race or completing a certain event. Example career goals include "Qualify for and run XYZ marathon", "Run a sub-3-hour marathon" or "Run a marathon every year".

Race Day Goal Setting

Examples of medium-term goals include "Race a 10K in under 40 minutes by January" or "Win my age group in my next race." Professional runner Deena Kastor arrived at the 2009 Bank of America Chicago Marathon with ambitious goals: Victory and a sub-2:20 finishing time. "My preparations had gone well and I hadn't put together two months of quality work like I did for Chicago in a very long time. I felt on top of my game physically and mentally," said Kastor, the American record-holder (2:19:36, London 2006). Kastor felt strong throughout the race, which was her first marathon since she'd suffered a broken foot during the 2008 Olympic marathon and failed to finish. She finished sixth in a time of 2:28:50. As Kastor saw it, her goals had still served a vitally important purpose. "The trick is striving for the goal, but being grateful for the progress if you don't happen to reach it,"[1] she said.

Once you've set your goals, don't focus on them. Focus on the process of training instead. Focusing on the process means concentrating on the steps you must take to improve each day, as opposed to

---

[1] Running Times Magazine by Jonathan Beverly (Editor-in-Chief)

focusing on the end goal itself. Process goals focus on actual acts of performance and learning, such as setting the goal of decreasing your split times; whereas product goals focus on the outcome of the performance, such as winning a race. Examples of process goals include "Run 5 days and 60 km this week" or "Run one speed workout per week". The difference between the two is subtle, but important. Runners who train solely to achieve a product goal tend to push harder and increase training volume without regard to the feedback their body is providing, resulting in inconsistent training, stagnant results, and even injury. Mentally tough athletes are process-oriented.

You might set specific training goals as follows:

- Total number of kilometers per week that you want to build up to;
- average weekly kilometers for each of the different running methods, such as general aerobic endurance, tempo running, specialized endurance, and anaerobic endurance;
- paces (minutes per kilometer or mile) for running methods;
- longest continuous aerobic run and tempo run to be attempted;
- average weekly loads of fundamental training such as circuit, weight, and technique training.

If you are motivated and committed enough to

endure hard training, then you will be a tough competitor when racing. Include time trials and other tests in your training to provide opportunities to build your self-confidence. By setting and achieving progressively more challenging goals, you will develop confidence. A runner must have confidence; typically, runners who under-perform are lacking confidence. Building confidence takes time and is something to work on leading up to the race. Recognizing your strengths is part of that process.

The final step in effective goal setting is the continual evaluation of your progress and the setting of new goals. At the end of each run, each training period, after races, after injuries and at the end of a season or year are all good times to evaluate your progress toward reaching your goals. Considering the experiences of the previous period, you can reset your long- and short-term goals to guide you to success. A good example of this is when coming back from an injury. Many runners who have to take time off to heal from an injury immediately return to hard training in an attempt to achieve their goal. They risk getting injured again so that they can "make up time". The problem with this approach is that it often leads to further injury. A better approach in this situation is to put your pre-injury goals on hold and focus on taking the next logical step in your training each week. Increase your volume only by as much as your body is ready to handle and train to your current fitness level, not where you were before your injury or where you want to be on race day. This logical progression might not allow you to hit your goal on race day, but you'll have months of consistent training behind you and, most importantly, you'll be healthy and ready to keep training hard for the next race. And there will always be other races.

When Goal Setting Doesn't Work

Goal setting is an effective motivator of behavior that leads to improved performance, but there are common pitfalls that can interfere with the effectiveness of your goal setting. The two most critical pitfalls relate to the plan designed to achieve the goal. The failure to devise a plan for achieving a goal is a major pitfall. Setting a goal without designing a plan to achieve the goal is like making a wish. The second major pitfall is not following the plan once it has been devised. Step 1 is to set a measurable goal. Step 2 is to devise a plan to achieve the goal. Step 3 is to follow the plan.

Focus on the process, train consistently, stay healthy, and keep moving towards your goals one day at a time.

CHAPTER SIX

Using a Reward System

"Exercise is the best mood booster in the world, at least for me! I view it as me time. For example, when I am feeling down, the workout tends to bring me back to a positive place. It also makes my body feel fantastic, which reduces all sorts of stress. All the way around, working out makes my life so much better." - Kate MacKenzie

"I continue to be amazed at the effect of exercise on my mood. Even just a short amount can greatly increase my energy levels and general happiness. Now that I'm not competing, it can be hard to convince myself to go for a workout, but it's worth it every time." – Olympic Rower

"My reward for a workout is getting a shower and feeling good about myself for the rest of the day." – Gary W. Hall

Sometimes it's hard to get yourself out the door to run. Relying on willpower doesn't always work. We tell ourselves we will make ourselves do it, but that puts a lot of strain on our willpower resources, and everyone's willpower is a limited resource. Once your resolve is weakened--when you're tired or stressed, and you're tempted by distractions that are more appealing than running--willpower breaks down. A reward system is helpful for those times when intrinsic motivation alone is not sufficient to get you out running. Reward systems are a form of extrinsic motivation. For runners, external rewards might be top finishes in a race, awards, prize money, sponsorship or fame. The ultimate outcome, not necessarily the training and racing, drive extrinsically-motivated individuals to excel. The following powerful reward system is already biologically programmed into your body. You just need to become conscious of it.

One Run Away From a Good Mood

One strategy to motivate yourself to run is to focus on mood rewards. Here, the focus is not on feeling good at some point in the future but on feeling good now. You don't have to wait months for the positive effects of running, as you would in the case of weight-loss goals. You can feel very differently in as little as half an hour. And high intensity running is not required to bring about mood changes. Moderate intensity is adequate for mood benefit. Actually, moderate rather than high-intensity running is easier to maintain over time. As you run for mood, you will be constantly reminded of the benefit you are producing. And the positive feeling appears to be a universal emotion experienced after exercise. From population-based studies to clinical trials, powerful evidence suggests that exercise can have substantial effects on mood, lifting everyday bad moods and feelings of stress, as well as offering treatment effects for diagnosed depression that rival antidepressant medications. A study summarizing 70 studies of this topic showed that adults who experienced sad or depressed moods, but not at levels that met criteria for a psychiatric disorder, reliably reported meaningful improvements in their mood as they started exercising. Exercise helps restore a normal mood; it refreshes you emotionally.

To use mood rewards as a motivation to run, it is important to maximize the link between a run and enjoying the associated mood benefits. You run to feel less stressed, less down, and more relaxed. You run for the sense of energy it provides and for the sense of being in tune with your body. When feeling demoralized about running, remind yourself of its utility. Remember that negative feelings are never a reason to avoid exercise; they are the reason to exercise. A bad mood before running often means that you will experience bigger mood gains from the run. As such, skipping a run because of a bad mood is like skipping an aspirin when you have a headache. Remind yourself that running is your break, a chance to clear your head and reset your mood. Keep this in mind as you think about the next run. The more you notice and review these benefits, the tighter the linkage between process and goal will be, and the easier it will be to run the next time.

Another type of reward that you can use to motivate yourself to run is a financial reward. People are significantly more likely to stick with an exercise program when there are financial rewards for doing so. That's true even if the amount of money is small, according to a 2013 study published in the American Journal of Preventative Medicine. Researchers looked at 11 studies that examined if giving people financial incentives would increase their participation in exercise programs. Eight of the 11 studies found that financial incentives were associated with an 11.55% increase in exercise session participation. The effectiveness of financial incentives was greater in programs that included objective measurements of physical activity and those that offered assured rewards rather than "lottery-style" rewards. The amount of financial reward offered ranged from $2.79 to $46.82 per week. While larger amounts appeared to yield bigger results, even modest incentives of about $5 a week were associated with increased exercise participation.

Rewards can be as varied as the individuals who appreciate them: clothes, shoes, a book, a DVD. Reward yourself with small items for small improvements in your performance; save the bigger rewards for when you achieve significant time or distance goals. Laying out cash for a new running jacket, compression socks, or that sweet GPS watch can perk up your training because you'll want to get your money's worth. Purchasing high-quality shoes and gear tends to make you feel more self-confident and more committed to your training. A runner I know puts one dollar into a jar after every run, and occasionally rewards herself by buying something with the money. Set a performance goal and a reward for attaining that goal. Running a certain distance and finishing a specific distance in a specific time are examples of performance goals. I use a token system to motivate myself to run, and give myself extra tokens for beating my P.R. and average time for a certain route. After I acquire a certain number of tokens I reward myself by buying something that I want. Even better: Reward yourself immediately. Right after your run, treat yourself to something you genuinely enjoy--a hot shower, a soak, a massage--so your brain associates exercise with an immediate reward.

A Note of Caution: Avoid Compensatory Behaviors

Be wary of compensatory eating and sitting after running. Be particularly vigilant of the tendency to use food as a reward for running. By this I mean the subtle decisions of how you load up your plate during meals, or whether you select an extra dessert during the day because you went for a run. Unfortunately, compensatory eating is common in the running community. Giving in to this hedonic urge has been shown to nullify the expected weight-loss benefits of the run. You should also be wary of compensatory sitting--the tendency to sit more during the day because you went for a run. For some, additional sitting is seen as a reward for running ("I ran this morning, I might as well take it easy now"); for others, it may be a reaction to feeling fatigued ("I should relax to recover").

CHAPTER SEVEN

The Nature of Performance Anxiety

"Once you're beat mentally, you might as well not even go to the starting line." - Todd Williams

How do you feel as you toe the starting line at a race? If you're like most runners, you feel intense anxiety. Internal alarms are going off. Every runner has experienced pre-race anxiety, and most have let it affect their performance. Anxiety isn't necessarily a bad thing, because it means you care about your performance. Speaking of racing, Olympian Michael Johnson said "I felt nervous, sure, but I needed to. When the nerves came I was pleased because I know I need to be a little nervous to bring out the best in me. So I kind of register the nerves and then use them to focus.'' However, your instinctive effort to protect yourself from perceived threat or the expectation of threat may make you lose sight of why you're running. You lose your focus often without even realizing it. You're as scared of the possibility of success as you are by the possibility of failure. Running fast is as fear inducing as running slowly. Or perhaps you're frightened of losing control of your body when tired. Most importantly, you're unaware of these influences that affect you. These influences include self-defeating behaviors such as inadequate or excessive warm-ups, poor pacing, and inattentiveness to running form.

These performance anxieties that swallow us are the modern byproducts of the archaic fears of disapproval, rejection, envy, abandonment and annihilation. Most psychologists divide anxiety into two types: somatic and cognitive. Somatic anxiety refers to physical manifestations: butterflies in the stomach, increased heart rate, and other signs. Cognitive anxiety refers to activity of the mind: negative thoughts, low self-esteem, and others. A little analysis of this type can be useful because the methods used to combat cognitive and somatic anxiety are very different. For example, in case of nerves you'll invariably hear the advice, "Take some deep breaths." This is helpful if the problem is somatic, because deep breaths slow the heart rate, but it'll do little for cognitive anxiety. Meditation or other relaxation techniques are effective against somatic, or physical, anxiety symptoms, but do little to combat cognitive anxiety and the wasted energy used by excessive mental processing.

The key to managing these performance anxieties is to disarm the alarms. By controlling your emotional thermostat you preclude the need to defend against it in self-defeating ways. Stay calm and you won't have to deploy self-defeating strategies in search of calm.

In this state of focused readiness, you can know the difference between what is inside you, outside you, and what has already happened versus what may occur. What are the real and the perceived emotional risks of giving your best effort? In a state of maintained centeredness, you can know the difference. Distancing your current effort from the expectations and results of previous efforts, most often you can see the current risks as reasonable and justified.

Research shows that meditation and visualization are effective strategies to mediate performance anxieties--both are elements of mental rehearsal. Remembering the past creates our anxieties and imagining the future can dismantle them. The following chapters detail how to manage your performance anxiety.

CHAPTER EIGHT

How to Talk to Yourself About Running

"The ultra distance leaves you alone with your thoughts to an excruciating extent. Whatever song you have in your head had better be a good one. Whatever story you are telling yourself had better be a story about going on. There is no room for negativity. The reason most people quit has nothing to do with their body." - Scott Jurek

"Running is nothing more than a series of arguments between the part of your brain that wants to stop and the part that wants to keep going." - Unkown author

A common problem in running is engaging in self-statements that reveal unpleasant feelings about running. Amateur and recreational runners are especially susceptible to engaging in self-deprecating thinking; "I'm a slow runner" or "I don't even know if I'm going to finish" are common examples. A similar problem is The Comparison Trap: comparing yourself with other runners. This can create

43

frustration and a negative outlook. Negative self-comparison is especially common in young runners. There's nothing wrong with aspiring to be as good a runner as a teammate or opponent or even a champion. But if that aspiration makes you feel inferior and leads you to downplay your own abilities, it's detrimental. This behavior, especially if continued during training and competition, will likely lead to declining motivation, reduced effort, and even dropping out. If you're negative and lack self-confidence throughout your training, no amount of pre-race self-talk and mental preparation is going to undo weeks or months of self-deprecation.

Reframing your belief in yourself must start in training. "Re-framing" is an important concept in psychology; it means changing the perspective from which you look at something. You can conquer your self-doubt by re-framing your thoughts. First, identify your negative thoughts. This isn't easy as negative thoughts are insidious. "I always get tired at this point," or "I never run well in the morning" are examples. Even the weather can spur a chain of performance-hampering thoughts. If you think "It's going to be hot out today" you plant a seed before you get started that the run is going to be lousy. In response to a negative thought, use thought-stopping. Say "negative thought", "not now", "stop!", or something similar to yourself (even picture a stop sign if it helps). The effect is that the negative thought usually goes away. The command will remind you of the unpleasant effects of the thoughts, and allow you to regain the proper mental state for a more positive message. Note the negative thoughts that occur before and during your runs, and write them in your running journal.

A good mental conditioning program should also teach you to avoid "don't thinking", which are an ineffective series of thoughts in which you focus on what you don't want to do. "Don't screw this up, don't start too fast, don't get caught in the pack..." Instead, focus on process goals. Specific things you need to do during a run or race in order to be effective.

"Or-thinking" can also make running more difficult. Consider these examples of "Or-thinking":

- I can feel tired OR I can have a good run.
- I can be struggling OR I can enjoy the benefits of running.

Now substitute "and" for "or" in your thinking, and consider the new perspective:

- I can feel really tired AND I can have a good run.
- I can be struggling AND I can enjoy the benefits of running.

Seemingly opposite emotions can co-exist side by side. Your task is to develop a frame of mind that allows you to enjoy running, even with the experience of exertion or fatigue. Be open and light--open to embracing the good parts of the experience, even when the other parts of the experience are taxing. By not joining with the most negative parts of your running experience, and instead relaxing with your exertion, you will feel lighter on your runs.

The above examples of negative thinking are all judgements. Judgement results in tightness, which interferes with the fluidity required for smooth running. Relaxation produces smooth running, and results from accepting your running as it is, even if flawed. It is important to learn to let go of the human inclination to judge ourselves, our performance or experience, as good or bad. These self-judgments usually become self-fulfilling prophecies. You become what you think you are. Letting go of judgments does not mean ignoring weaknesses. It simply means seeing events as they are and not adding to them. This can be done by using descriptive but nonjudgmental words to describe the events you see.

Positive messages are provided by positive self-talk (PST). In a 1977 study, Michael Machoney, Ph.D. and M. Avener, Ph.D. found that athletes who made the U.S. men's gymnastics team used more positive self-talk than those who didn't. Based on their comprehensive study of Olympic gymnasts, they reported in a 1992 paper that the more positive an athlete's self-talk, the easier it is for the athlete to excel. PST is now a universal practice among elite runners. When PST is used to gain or to maintain self-confidence, focusing inwardly and thinking about one's strengths rather than about one's weaknesses or opponents, it can generate a sense of self-control and responsibility for a race's outcome. PST is the primary antidote to anxious thoughts, low confidence, self-doubt, and other forms of negative mood state. It improves the psychological readiness to perform under pressure. PST is easy to do and will help you to focus and feel relaxed and confident. It involves substituting positive, or at least neutral, thoughts for your negative thoughts. It's not necessary to tell yourself "I'm the fastest runner in the world and I feel great today"; you can't lie to yourself. Just take the thought one step in the positive direction. Change "I don't think I can finish" to "I can make it to the next landmark". This is known as incremental coping. It's important not to let yourself start thinking "It's over. There's nothing I can do" or "I'm out of it." Instead, say to yourself "I still have a chance. Everyone else must be feeling as bad as me," or "I've trained long and hard for this, and I'm not going to let it slip away now," or "This race isn't over. I can gut it out. I've done this before and I can do it again. I can still get back into it." Your substituted thoughts should be positive, truthful, and relevant.

You also should use positive self-talk after running well. For example, say to yourself after running well "Good work. That's me. That's how I'm capable of running", to yourself after running well, for example. This type of response builds confidence. After running poorly, tell yourself something positive, such as, "That's not me. I can run better than that." Don't dwell on the poor performance.

When to Talk to Yourself About Running

In addition to being physically demanding, training can become a mental burden. Many runners spend too much of their time thinking about training. They spend hours analyzing previous training sessions, worrying about their upcoming workouts, fretting over unachieved goals, fearing the pain they are experiencing, or worrying about their diet. An effective way to overcome this worry is to compartmentalize your running. Think of it as you are putting your training in a locker, separating it from your life outside running. An example of running compartmentalization is using an hour before and an hour after each run to think about running. The hour before the run provides enough time to get mentally prepared, and the hour after a run provides sufficient time to recover and reflect. Don't allow yourself to think about running outside this time period. Of course, it will take several weeks before you stop ruminating about your training. But this practice will get easier over time until it becomes second nature. When it does, you will perform better during workouts and gain more enjoyment from running.

Using Mantras to Become a Better Runner

In a 2013 study, 24 recreational cyclists rode as long as they could at 80% of their peak power output, and their times were recorded. Subjects were then divided into two groups. One group was given instruction in motivational self-talk. The other received no mental training. Two weeks later, the cyclists repeated the time-to-exhaustion test. Riders who had received self-talk instruction were reminded to use the four statements ("mantras") they had selected during their mental training instruction (phrases such as "feeling good," "drive forward," and "push through this"). The control group was given no motivational instruction. The cyclists who used self-talk reported a nearly 1-point drop on a 10-point scale of perceived exertion and improved their time by 18%. No significant changes in perceived effort or time were recorded by the control group. Self-talk has been an effective sports psychology tool for years, but this study is the first to show a direct link between the mantras we repeat to ourselves and their influence on how we feel--and on whether we keep going.

Running mantras (also called "power words") are phrases or words that you repeat mentally while you are running in order to achieve a certain state or goal. "Mantra" is a Sanskrit word that literally means "instrument for thinking." These words or short phrases have long been used to focus the mind in meditation. A mantra can help keep your mind off the difficulty of running, keep you going, and keep you focused on a performance goal. An effective mantra addresses what you want to feel, not the adversity you're trying to overcome. A good mantra is short, positive, instructive, and full of action words. My favorites are "Mindfulness" and "Finish on empty."

Try some of the following mantras. Modify them to suit your taste, if necessary.

THE RESILIENT RUNNER

Everyday Mantras

- I can do this.
- I am a runner.
- Born to run.
- O2, CO2, O2, CO2 ... (oxygen, carbon dioxide ...)
- In, out, in, out ...

Mantras for Tough Times

- This will pass.
- The base is there, use it.
- Strong. Confident. Relaxed.
- Keep going, lion (Kenyan mantra).

Mantras for Slow Days

- Completing is succeeding.
- No need for speed, just finish.
- All Ks are good Ks (All miles are good miles).
- Just one K 5** times. (**insert your number)
- Gut it out.

Mantras for Racing

- Well prepared.
- Race my pace.
- Stay on pace.
- Calm, focused, strong, steady-paced.
- Run my race.
- I'm killing it.

- Tougher than the rest.
- The strong get stronger.
- Finish strong.

Mantras of Famous Athletes

- "Find a way," used by Diana Nyad, who completed a record-breaking 53-hour swim from Cuba to the U.S.
- "This is what you came for," used by ultra-marathon runner Scott Jurek.
- "Do what I can do in this moment," used by Dave Scott, a six-time Ironman triathlon world champion.
- "Relentless!" used by Bill Rodgers, American national distance running hall of famer.
- "Define yourself," "Go faster" and "Push harder", used by Deena Kastor, Olympic bronze medalist, U.S. women's marathon record holder.
- "Stay focused," "Run hard," and "Make yourself breathe," used by Alan Culpepper, 2004 U.S. Olympic trials marathon champion.

Ultra-distance runner Anne Lundblad describes her experience at the 2005 World Cup 100K: "I went out too fast and didn't drink enough for what turned out to be a hot day, and by 30 kilometers, I was exhausted, dizzy, experiencing GI problems and seriously contemplating a DNF. I talked to the team doc, who advised me to slow down, drink something and continue onward. I followed his advice and also began to repeat the mantra I had used in training: 'I'm healthy, strong and tough'. Miraculously, things began to turn around. I regained my energy and motivation, picked up the pace, and began to pass people, ultimately ending up with the silver medal and a P.R." [2]

Distance runners are especially exposed to fear and doubt. The longer the event, the more time you have to think and worry. Long distances require a lot of self-discipline, because there's so much training involved. Many distance runners are perfectionists: their minds tend to look at what should have been better, and worry about potential adversity. One of the keys to confidence is to recall your performance accomplishments. Success boosts confidence. To ensure that you have a confident outlook before running a race, count up the training kilometers that you ran in the months before the event. Write the number big and bold on your arm and look at it while running. Make the number into a mantra and repeat it to yourself while running.

If these mantras don't work for you then create your own. One way to develop your mantras is to remember thoughts you have while running well. If you're feeling especially strong or light on your feet, recognize those sensations and try to translate them into a mantra. Write down your post-run thoughts in your journal. You may find a pattern of things that occur when you're doing well. Mantras may emerge

---

[2] Running Times Magazine by Jonathan Beverly (Editor-in-Chief)

that will help you replicate that optimal state.

It's best to have a stash of phrases that you can call upon based on your mood or run. You want to produce different sensations depending on what you have to overcome. On a long run you might want a phrase that keeps your pace steady and helps you to endure the distance. When you are racing a 5K, on the other hand, you might want to switch to something that will help you push harder and tap your inner speed demon. Another advantage to having a stash of mantras is that tried-and-true mantras may not work on every run. Giving yourself orders that you physically can't obey is more likely to discourage you than move you. Telling yourself something that you don't believe isn't going to help. You cannot lie to yourself successfully. Instead, focus on things you can control ("one foot in front of the other," "run tall," or "breathe easy," for example). These messages can ease performance-related stress and relax your body, helping you run better.

Another strategy for using mantras is to print out a map of the course you intend to run and write down what you want to think at each marker. Having mantras planned out can give you the mental edge to persist when negative thoughts creep into your mind as your body begins to fatigue. Use mantras to refute those negative thoughts and push past tired legs. Anticipate the negative feelings and think positive thoughts instead.

Think strong words, repeat an inspiring phrase,

and run better. Use mantras to help carry you forward to whatever your running goals might be.

CHAPTER NINE

The Mindful Runner

Focus

"A large part of my attraction to running was its meditative qualities - the calming process of quiet, deep-thought, long-distance running allows for. I enjoyed not only a physical 'high' from the exercise, but an emotional release as well." - Jacine Harrington

"I find significance in all kinds of small details when I run; I'm hyper aware of my surroundings, the sensations in my body, and the thoughts running through my mind." - Sakyoung Mipham

When athletes are having a great performance, they're focused solely on the present moment. They aren't thinking about the past or the future. This way of thinking is often called "being in the zone". However, giving your complete and undivided attention to a task is challenging. The skill of fully attending to the task at hand and excluding internal distractions and irrelevant external cues must be learned.

Focus Styles

A focus style is a preference for paying attention to certain cues. Athletes tend to be more comfortable focusing on some cues and ignoring others. Every athlete has a dominant style that impacts all aspects of her performance. This dominant style will surface most noticeably when the athlete is under pressure. Two types of focus styles--internal and external— exist.

Internal focus style
Runners with an internal focus style perform best when they're totally and consistently focused on running during training and racing. They keep their focus narrow, thinking only about running. These athletes tend to be easily distracted by activity in their immediate surroundings. If they broaden their focus and take their mind off running, for example, by talking about non-running topics with a coach or fellow runner during training, they'll become distracted and will have trouble narrowing their focus back onto running.

External focus style
Runners with an external focus style perform best when they only focus on running only when they're about to begin training or a race. At other times it is best for them to broaden their focus and take their

minds off running. These runners have a tendency to think too much, become negative and critical, and experience competitive anxiety. For these runners, it's essential that they take their focus away from running when they're not actually running.

Understanding your focus style is essential to managing it. Are you a runner who needs to keep your mind on running in order to perform well? Or are you someone who thinks too much and needs to keep your mind off running until it's time to perform? The ability to manage your focus is most important in races. There is a tendency for runners under pressure to revert to a focus style that interferes with rather than helps their performance. If you're someone who performs best with an external focus style, for example, you may find yourself turning your focus inward when the pressure is on; this will result in you thinking too much and becoming anxious. In this situation it would be best for you to turn your focus outward by looking around and taking your mind off running. Generally, when you lose your prime focus style under pressure, you should take steps to redirect your focus back to the style that works best for you.

As a runner, you can easily become distracted by the following obstacles.

External distractions may involve heavy traffic getting to a competition, competitors, or equipment problems.

Internal distractions for athletes include self-doubt, fears, expectations, and fatigue. These include:

Thinking about the outcome. This is probably the greatest obstacle to focus in all sports. You race because you want to win, but this focal point is one of the greatest causes of poor performance and loss.

Becoming too emotional while competing. When your emotional level becomes too high, your concentration level drops. When you become too emotional, two major things occur. Your body changes in a negative way. Your muscles tighten, your heart rate increases, you have shallow breathing; and your focus becomes clouded. You're thinking about being excited or nervous (or even angry or happy) instead of focusing on what it takes to perform well.

How to Overcome Obstacles to Focus

To overcome the outcome obstacle, train yourself to focus on the process--the specific skills you're performing. You control the process. When you focus on the process and not the outcome, you dramatically increase your chances of success.

The emotion obstacle can be overcome by becoming more aware of your emotional arousal levels. Know the warning signs that you're becoming too emotional: faster heart rate, shakiness, jittery hands or legs, a knot in your stomach, racing thoughts, and muscle tightness.

Exercises to Develop Focus

Focus is a skill like any other, which means you can learn it and get better at it with practice. Here are some ways to improve focus:

Take regular inventories of body cues such as breathing rate, muscle tightness, the sound of your footstrike, and running technique. These cues tell you how hard you are working, and help you adjust your effort to save energy and improve technique. Heavy, plodding footstrikes indicate that your form is breaking down. If you sense too much tension in your shoulders, for example, you can consciously relax these muscles.

Practice running in a crowd. Running in a pack challenges you to shift focus from your positioning (to avoid tripping and running too wide on curves) to cues that indicate how your competitors are doing. By listening to the breathing rate of other runners, you can tell whether they're having trouble with the pace. Running in a pack also helps you to relax and move along with the flow of your competitors without being distracted. When the pace is fast and steady, running in a pack gives runners a tremendous advantage; the runners work together and pull each other along. However, it takes considerable skill in focusing attention and maintaining relaxation to gain this advantage.

Sometimes, however, the pack gets away, so it's also important to practice running alone. If you run in for a club or team, the leader or coach can stagger runners during training sessions so that runners can practice running alone. These sessions will challenge you to keep your focus open, staying in mental contact with those ahead of you. Mental contact refers to the feeling that even though your competitors are ahead you have the energy, confidence, and focus to not let them get away.

Plan and visualize. Write in your journal about the specific situations when you lost your focus. Come up with a plan for how a composed runner would handle such situations, and then use imagery to see yourself managing them in this productive way. Planning and visualization will help you maintain your focus when these situations arise in the future. (See Chapter 10: Visualization for further details.)

Meditation

One way to train the mind is through the practice of meditation. Many runners say that running is their "meditation." But running only works with the periphery or superficial level of thoughts, concerns, and worries. Unless we train it, the mind does the minimum necessary to fulfill a function. Meditation doesn't just deal with the periphery of thoughts; it goes all the way to their core. The practice of meditation involves spending time in quiet non-thought.

To practice meditation you should find a quiet

setting where you can sit undisturbed for 20-30 minutes. To avoid inhibiting circulation, loose clothing is advisable. There are several positions (sitting, standing, walking, and lying down) but the sitting position is most conducive to staying alert and relaxed. There are several sitting positions: Burmese Style, Half Lotus, Full Lotus, Seiza Position, and chair sitting. I just sit on the floor with my legs extended straight in front of me. I recommend beginning meditation in 20 minute sessions; I use the digital watch that I use on my runs as a timer. I also recommend keeping your eyes closed, though you can meditate with your eyes open. This is usually done with your gaze resting on the floor about a meter in front of you. Keep your mouth closed, and breathe through your nose. Pressing the tongue against the upper palate will reduce the need to salivate and swallow.

What you do with your mind, not what you do with your body, is most important. In order to stay concentrated in the present you must concentrate on an object or activity that is always present. What is more present than one's breathing? Putting attention on breathing simply means observing your breath going in and out. It does not mean intentionally controlling your breath. When the mind is fastened to the rhythm of breathing, it tends to become absorbed and calm. The breath is always present, and if the mind is focused on breathing it won't wander into the past or future. Listening to your breathing can be effective in blocking out nervousness and other irrelevant objects of attention. The practice of this exercise will enable you to achieve deeper and deeper states of concentration. Most runners who practice breath-following as a discipline find it helpful almost immediately.

When the inevitable thought comes to mind say "Not now, thought," and re-focus your mind on your breathing. In the beginning stages of meditation especially you will find it challenging to control your mind. Strangely, even when you have experienced the practical benefit of a still mind, you will continue to find it an elusive state. You will find your mind wandering again and again. The mind has difficulty focusing on a single object for an extended period of time. The greatest lapses in concentration come when you allow your mind to project what is about to happen or to dwell on what has already happened. The mind easily absorbs itself in the world of "what if?" However, meditation will become easier as you practice. No one would think they could walk out the door one day and run a marathon, so you should not expect to meditate for 15 minutes and begin feeling peace. Just as in running, you have to train. You train your mind to get used it to being more peaceful and less attached to its thoughts. In meditation you are developing the ability to think when you want to, and to not think when you don't want to. Meditation changes the rhythm of brain activity. Specifically, it induces a rhythmical pattern of neural firing known as the alpha-wave state, which is associated with feelings of calmness and wellbeing. Once meditation has brought confidence to your mind, you will be able to practice mindfulness in almost any circumstance.

You will feel a certain equanimity even in challenging environments. When you are neither threatened nor seduced by external distractions, you can naturally relax almost anywhere, resting in a deeper consciousness and a more mindful mind, because you are fully present.

Meditation will help you to avoid injuries while running because it puts you in tune with your body and makes you aware of your surroundings. It can also help you perform better by giving you more control over your thoughts. Meditation can also help you get through a training program by preventing you from becoming overwhelmed by worries, doubts, or other negative thoughts. Aches and pains are common when running regularly. But if you work with the mind through meditation, you will not let these pains deflate you and destroy your confidence.

The longer you can focus on one thing, the more successful you can be at focusing in mentally tough situations while running. Practice this focusing exercise each day while running and you'll find you are running faster and with more enjoyment.

Mindfulness

We runners tend to zone out during runs, taking our minds away from their physical activity. When that happens, our bodies and minds have separated, and, like most divorces, it is not a happy one. Our minds are constantly producing thoughts, and it is often surprising how random, bizarre, and even how negative some of these thoughts are. Our minds darting here and there actually weigh on us physically. A wandering mind is the kiss of death to your race. Let those middle miles slip by in a mental fog and the body starts running on autopilot; as you tire the pace starts to lag and by the time you finally come to you've already been beaten. In a marathon, the middle kilometers 21-32 (miles 13-20) are when many runners check out mentally. That attention lapse leads to precious time and places lost from your performance.

Instead of zoning out, do the opposite: Practice mindfulness. Mindfulness is a common stress-reduction technique with Buddhist roots. In mindfulness, you train your ability to focus on something and stay with it. You are exercising a muscle of the mind. In the beginning, you will be like a child at the gym, only able to hold the lightest dumbbells for a few seconds. When your mind is distracted, you drop the weight. But if you keep exerting yourself and increasing the weight, your body becomes stronger. Similarly, the more you exercise your mindfulness, the stronger it becomes. Mindfulness can be used like a kite string to keep your mind from following the winds of thought, which are often unfriendly during runs. Quieting the mind means less thinking, calculating, judging, worrying, fearing, hoping, and regretting. The mind is still when it is totally present in perfect oneness with the running and the runner. Quieting the mind is a gradual process involving the learning of several inner skills. The inner skills are really arts of forgetting mental habits acquired since we were children. The first skill to learn is the art of letting go of the human inclination to judge ourselves and our running as good or bad.

A 2013 University of California at San Diego study contains evidence of the effectiveness of mindfulness in increasing endurance. Martin Paulus and his colleagues studied elite performers such as Navy SEALS and top multi-day adventure racers. A group of SEAL recruits took a standard eight-week mindfulness course, and brain scans showed they developed some of the same brain patterns that hardened SEALs and adventure racers had displayed. The changes persisted even a year later.

To apply mindfulness to running, you should avoid daydreaming, problem solving and listening to music while running. Music can make you oblivious to important clues,such as that oncoming car, or your body's signals (your body may be trying to tell you that you are going too fast, for example). You can also become dependent on music--which is not a good thing if your device's battery goes dead mid-run or if you plan to race without it. Instead, plug into yourself. The interior world is a natural antidote to the boredom you may experience on a run (especially while running on a treadmill). Initiate your runs, and your mindfulness, by focusing on your breathing. Is it shallow or deep? Is it smooth or rough? Rough or coarse breathing could mean that you are tired or overworked, or that there is some conflict in your life.

Smooth or gentle breathing might indicate harmony, relaxation, or other positive feelings. During another portion of your run focus on your footfall. Are you landing on the heel, the midsection, or the ball of your foot? Listen to your footfall. Listen to the rhythm of your breathing and footfall. Meditative running is an extension of the basic meditation practice that is performed while sitting, which teaches you to keep your mind focused on your breathing, or following each breath as it flows out of your lungs. When your mind becomes distracted by other thoughts, acknowledge it and return your focus to your breath and footfall.

Keep in mind that running has many distractions: traffic, pedestrians, and terrain concerns, to name a few--that make it difficult to continuously focus on one thing. It's almost impossible to be present the entire time while you run. But on a forty-five minute run, for example, staying focused for even fifteen minutes is beneficial to the body and mind. I know of no better way to deal with anxiety than to focus the mind on one's breathing process. Anxiety is fear about what may happen in the future, and it occurs when the mind is imagining what the future may bring. But when your attention is on the present, the actions one must do in the present have their best chance of being successfully accomplished. By letting go of thoughts and coming back to your immediate physical experience, you will find that our body softens and your mind feels lighter, more joyful. Such mindfulness brings satisfaction and contentment. In this healthy state, the mind is more likely to generate positive thoughts. You will feel more at ease and happier.

CHAPTER TEN

Visualization

"Visualize this thing that you want, see it, feel it, believe in it. Make your mental blueprint, and begin to build." – Robert Collier

Many runners prepare physically before every race but are discouraged to discover that this is not sufficient to win the race, win their age group, or beat their P.R. The factor they are missing is mental preparedness. To become mentally prepared, professional athletes now commonly use a tool called visualization. Visualization is the process of imagining a future event happening in the present; that is, you watch something in your mind before actually doing it. Research confirms that visualization is a powerful tool in athletics. In 1988, Canadian sport psychologists Terry Orlick, Ph.D., and John Partington, Ph.D., found that 99% of the 235 athletes they surveyed relied on this technique to prepare for a high stakes race. A 2010 study examining the relationship between mental toughness and imagery use found that the athletes who scored highest for mental toughness were those who most often used mental imagery. The Canadian researchers studied 151 college varsity athletes. Those who scored highest for mental toughness were much more likely to practice what the researchers call "motivational general-mastery imagery". That is, they regularly pictured themselves succeeding at their sport. Studies by the U.S. Olympic Training Center show that 94% of coaches use mental rehearsal for training and competition. Visualization has helped elite runners reach their full potential. American endurance runner Kate Fonshell calmed herself at the start of her Olympic trials race by imagining doing her strides, taking in the stadium, the finish line, and reviewing the entire race, lap by lap. Fonshell then ran to a first place finish to win the 1996 Olympic Trials 10,000 m in 32:37, earning a berth on the U.S. Olympic team. American national champion Ceci St. Geme says that visualization helped her realize her full potential. She mentioned hearing splits, feeling surges, and sensing other aspects of the race in explicit detail prior to her national championship-winning performance.

Why does Visualization Work?

How can a sensory experience that takes place entirely in our minds enhance our ability to perform? Here are three theories:

Symbolic learning: This theory states that imagery helps develop a mental blueprint by creating a motor program in our nervous system. Rehearsal of the sequence of movements involved in a task allows us to learn them symbolically; we then apply them when we go onto the field of competition.

Psychoneuromuscular reaction. This theory states that mental practice is effective because it produces very small muscle contractions similar to those involved in physical practice. The process suggests that images produced in the mind transmit electrical impulses to our muscles and tendons for the performance of an athletic exercise.

"Psyching up." An offshoot of the psychoneuromuscular theory, this theory states that the muscular activity associated with mental practice represents a level of overall arousal that may be optimal for athletic performance. In essence, mental practice sets up a certain amount of energy in the body that prepares us for athletic endeavors.

Four factors determine the quality of mental imagery: perspective, control, the number of senses employed, and speed. Perspective refers to where your "imagery camera" is when you visualize. The internal perspective (first person perspective) involves seeing yourself from inside your body looking out, as if you are actually running. The external perspective (third person perspective) involves seeing yourself from outside your body, as if watching a video of yourself running. Neither perspective is better than the other. Most people have a dominant perspective they're most comfortable with. Use the perspective that's most natural for you, and experiment with the other perspective to see if it helps you in a different way.

Control refers to how well you are able to visualize what you want to visualize. If a mistake occurs in your imagery, don't ignore it. If you do, you'll ingrain the image, which will hurt your performance. Instead, rewind the "imagery video", and edit it until you perform correctly.

The number of senses employed refers to how many senses you engage when you visualize. The best running imagery involves a multi-sensory reproduction of running. Duplicate the sights, sounds, physical sensations, thoughts, and emotions that you will experience in a race.

Last, speed refers to the speed of your imagery. The ability to adjust the speed of your imagery will enable you to use imagery to improve different aspects of your running. Slow motion is effective for focusing on technique. When you first begin visualizing, use a slow imagery speed, and see yourself running correctly. Then increase the speed until you are performing well at real-time speed.

Personal Highlight Reel

You can also employ visualization to create a mental highlight reel of your performance. This reel consists of a combination of highlights from your best performance or performances, and is used to build confidence. There are two options to consider when creating your personal highlight reel. The first is to identify your best race or training performance (the more recent the better). Remember the entire performance, and select three to five personal highlights from it. The second is to identify a few of your best performances and choose a combination of your best highlights from those performances. Choose three to five best personal highlights, each lasting between ten to twenty seconds. For either option, make sure you select a performance in which you felt great, played really well, and experienced a positive outcome. Arrange the highlights sequentially as they occurred and include as your last highlight the greatest moment you experienced in running. Once completed, replay your highlight reel in your mind before every competition.

The personal highlight reel allows you to use visualization to remember past successes. Visualization can also be used to create future best performances. Unfortunately, when it comes to endurance running, many sports psychologists get this type of visualization wrong. Sports psychology as it is commonly practiced is a form of positive psychology, based on happy talk and a can-do spirit. Positive psychology has its place, but the widely recommended technique of visualizing yourself performing perfectly in races and feeling awesome while running usually hinders performance because it sends you into races with unrealistic expectations. Going into races expecting to feel any better than wretched in pursuit of maximum performance is a form of self-sabotage. Imagine the difficult aspects of the race—you have a kilometer to go in a 5K and feel horrible, or 5 miles to go in a marathon and your legs are getting wobbly. Then visualize yourself persevering through these tough patches and achieving your goal. Expect every race to be torturous, and you will race better. Athletes and coaches in the previously-mentioned 2010 study believe that an athlete's familiarity with his sport, and the adversities of the sport, make the athlete mentally tougher. By recalling past challenges and picturing yourself overcoming them, you will be mentally tougher the next time you encounter those obstacles.

Here is a very simple example of guided visualization for a 5K race:

Imagine yourself at the track or course on which you will compete. You are wearing your shorts, track top, and running shoes. Your mind is on the race. Notice the environment: the weather, the sun, the clouds. Notice the other runners. Feel yourself being calm and confident, looking forward to running, knowing that you are well prepared, you have trained hard, and are ready.

Imagine yourself doing your normal warm-up routine. After completing your warm-up, imagine lining up at the start, and hearing the starter giving you the instructions. You notice your opponents, you are feeling anxious yet under control. You feel the adrenaline flowing through your body; your muscles are ready to go.

You stand at the starting line, feeling the familiar anxiousness that you feel before every race. The gun sounds and you take off, running and jostling for position, the pack continues to change and move as you run on; you take your time, staying relaxed and fluid. Someone bumps your shoulder but you keep your balance and form, watching the other runners out of the corner of your eye, keeping track of where they are. Your stride is smooth, you are centered and balanced, and feel the power and energy surging through your body.

At the first-mile marker you check your watch and find that you are on schedule. You begin to push a little harder, knowing this second mile is important, focusing on your form and your breathing. You pass a few runners, getting into a better position.

You pass the two-mile marker, and check your watch; you are ahead of schedule. You feel your legs pumping powerfully. You pass other runners, relaxing your hands and your upper body, breathing deeply. Your pace is fast.

In the last 800 meters you surge, reaching down deep inside yourself to tap into your reserve.

In the last 400 meters you kick into your highest gear, passing more runners, driving to the finish, and through the finish line, hearing the cheers of the crowd. You slow, catching your breath. Your side's heaving, you hear the congratulations of your family, friends and teammates.

To make your own visualization, add to the above visualization or follow these steps:

1. See, hear, and feel yourself performing your race.
2. Dictate into a recorder (smartphone, computer, etc.) every detail that you can see, hear, and feel. Begin with arriving at the event and your experience of it, including sounds, colors, smells, the crowd, the weather, your feelings and your mental state. Imagine yourself being relaxed, confident, powerful, and in control of your body and mind. Include the mantras that will help you during your run. Endurance running is too lengthy to visualize the entire performance, so imagine yourself performing in four or five key parts of the race (the start and finish are two obvious parts to choose).
3. Transcribe your recording from step 2.
4. Re-read your transcription, and edit it.
5. Dictate your script into your recorder.
6. Listen to the recorded visualization, and make changes to the script where needed. If you've made changes to the script, repeat step 5.

You should do 3-4 visualization sessions per week, and each session should last 10-15 minutes. Find a quiet place where you won't be interrupted. Listen to the finished recording and put yourself into the performance using all of your scenes. With repetition you will hone your skills, and will get more out of each session.

There are several benefits of visualization:

- It creates a positive mindset and body response: It helps you achieve a positive mindset before and during a race as you are able to visualize a goal and not think negative thoughts. The body responds in a positive way as a result.
- It reduces stress and negative body reactions, helping you to keep a calm mind and body. Blood flow and oxygen levels are kept at a balanced level. This helps to maintain relaxed muscles, and to avoid cramps and other health problems.
- It enhances focus, allowing you to focus on one thing at a time before the race. This improves your ability to keep your mind relaxed and not get distracted by other thoughts or runners.
- It increases self-confidence: As you visualize positive results, you begin to gain more self-confidence. You then reach speeds that were not possible before, which increases your confidence, and the cycle continues.

One problem with imagery is that, unlike physical training, the results aren't tangible. This problem can be overcome through your running journal. Keep logs of every visualization session that include a rating of the quality of the visualization, any thoughts and feelings that occur (positive or negative), problems that emerged, and what you need to work on for the next session.

The difference between best performances and

good performances lies within the thinking process, and visualization helps runners achieve those best performances.

CHAPTER ELEVEN

Make Friends With Pain

Being a distance runner is about handling pain. If you can't manage pain, you probably won't end up as a distance runner. "- Kara Goucher

"Every day I train mentally and physically to beat pain. You know, the guy who beats pain and is well prepared is the guy who will win. In a big marathon, the good runners have all trained and are prepared physically. It comes down to mental strength. Pain doesn't kill; the winner is the guy who resists pain and survives it." - Hendrick Ramaala

"Experience has taught me how important it is to keep going, focusing on running relaxed. Eventually pain passes and flow returns." - Frank Shorter

"Suffering is an extraordinary teacher." – Ryan Hall

"Pain is the purifier. Love pain. Embrace pain." – Percy Cerutty

Distance running is a painful sport; perhaps the most painful sport. This is a difficult concept for non-runners to understand. Runners are often asked, "Why would you put yourself through something that you know is going to hurt?" For us, pain is a fundamental part of the process. We like to feel our lungs burn a little and our quadriceps become fatigued. It's part of the feeling of being alive. The acceptance of suffering also represents a turning away from society's obsession with numbing pain or medicating every discomfort. We are saying, "I'm not satisfied with this anesthetized way of living." Long-distance races also serve as rites of passage. You go into a race with a sense of self, and in the process of encountering pain and suffering, you are forced to discover who you really are. What defines me? Am I able to tolerate pain? Am I able to endure? Am I a person who perseveres? Most emerge at the end a stronger person, and that's something they carry over into the rest of their lives.

The capacity to tolerate suffering is as critical to success in running as are the various components of physical fitness. Running performance is limited by suffering tolerance. In endurance racing, nobody is able to use 100 percent of his or her physical capacity. Research has shown that runners always finish races and time trials with some reserve capacity left over; the factor that prevents them from using that reserve capacity is the feeling of suffering. Runners always reach the limit of their tolerance for suffering before they reach the limit of their physical capacity;

hence the phenomenon of the "end spurt." A 1981 British Medical Journal study compared 3 groups: elite swimmers, club-level swimmers, and non-competitive athletes. It found enormous differences in pain tolerance. The elite athletes lasted far longer than the club athletes, who in turn lasted longer than the non-athletes. Put simply, the top athletes were willing and able to suffer more and for longer. The lesson here is that a runner with a greater suffering tolerance will typically out-perform a runner of equal physical ability but lesser suffering tolerance in races. The good news is that the capacity to tolerate suffering can be trained. The maximum amount of suffering that a runner is able to tolerate before slowing down is not fixed. It is influenced by a variety of factors, including experience, motivation, and perceived importance of the effort. That's one reason why we can run faster in races than in workouts--because we are motivated in races, we are able to tolerate a greater degree of suffering and therefore to run faster. In addition to cultivating motivation to suffer, preparing to suffer in the extreme is an effective way to maximize this capacity and thus run faster. If you expect your race goal to be difficult to achieve, you are likely to find yourself suffering less than expected in the race, and you will probably speed up. However, if you expect your race goal to be achieved relatively easily, you are likely to find yourself suffering more than expected in the race, and this unpleasant surprise will trigger a performance-limiting loss of will that you will find very difficult to overcome. Studies have shown that elite runners are remarkably adept at finding their optimal race pace by feel.

When asked how she copes with suffering, professional distance runner Kara Goucher said: "For me it's about being able to focus on all the positive things. When I'm running a marathon or another race or even a hard training session and I'm hurting, I pick out all the good things. When you're running, there are a million things telling you you can't do it. Your feet hurt, it's windy, someone else looks great... I try to find those few positive things that tell me I really can and focus on those. 'It hurts but I am running a great pace.' 'Maybe I am tired, but I still have control over my body.'"[3]

One of the biggest factors separating elite runners from other runners is pain tolerance. Elite runners have opened themselves up to the positive aspects of pain. In everyday life we are taught to negate or medicate any physical discomfort or pain. But the more you learn to embrace pain, the better you'll deal with it over time. If you expect and embrace suffering, you will do better than someone who's scared of it. Acceptance of pain is a competitive advantage. This view is echoed in the following views of two athletes. "When I am running well, pain is just another feeling, as in: Am I hot or cold? Is it quiet or loud in this room?," said Justin Freeman, a 14:52 5K runner and former Olympian in cross-country skiing. "Pain becomes an indicator of whether I have the fitness to continue at a given pace,

---

[3] Running Times Magazine by Jonathan Beverly (Editor-in-Chief)

not something that controls me." Tibetan religious leader and runner Sakyong Mipham said about pain: "One could say that life is at least 50 percent pain. If we do not relate to pain, we are not relating to half our life. Everything is fine when we are happy, but when we are in pain, we become petrified. The inability to relate to pain narrows our playing field. When we are able to work with pain and understand it, life becomes twice as interesting. Relating to pain makes us more fearless and happy. After I developed an enormous blister on my foot while running my first marathon, a few runners asked me how I had dealt with the pain. Some of them implied that I must have been doing some secret meditation to block it out. I explained to them that I was not blocking it out: I was paying attention to the pain, but at the same time I did not allow it to steal my mind. The pain was an important part of the reality, but worrying excessively was not going to accomplish anything."[4]

Science supports this view of pain. A series of studies used fentanyl, a potent, synthetic painkiller, to completely block pain signals from the lower body of cyclists. Cycling performance was found to be worse, because subjects felt no pain and thus started very fast, and then ended up bonking in the second half of the trial. Completely blocking off pain isn't beneficial because it deprives you of valuable pacing feedback.

Neither is focusing on pain a benefit. One study

---

[4] Running with the Mind of Meditation: Lessons for Training Body and Mind by Sakyong Mipham

on hitting the wall examined the effect of runner's thought patterns. The researchers classified thought patterns in two different ways. The first classification was whether the runners paid attention to themselves or to the outside world: inward vs. outward. The second classification was whether they paid attention to things relevant to the task at hand or not relevant: monitoring vs. distraction. There were four categories: inward monitoring, outward monitoring, inward distraction, and outward distraction. In this study, thought patterns did not predict who hit the wall. However, among runners who hit the wall, thought patterns did have an effect on how soon they hit the wall, and how long it lasted. Runners who engaged in too much inward monitoring hit the wall earlier and suffered from its effects longer. It's important to pay attention to how your body feels, but too much time spent examining how you feel can create problems you wouldn't otherwise notice. Feelings of discomfort and pain are related to what you pay attention to. If you focus on your thirst, soreness or pain they will become magnified. Of course, it's important to notice pain because it may be a signal that you need to slow down or change your running form. But, if you worry about the pain or panic as a result of it, you'll increase the activity in the emotional part of your brain and make the pain worse. It's better to practice mindfulness, and keep emotion out of it. Spending too much time on inward monitoring also means that you are spending less time on outward monitoring such as paying attention to your pace, the route, and the location of the next water station. Sometimes it's best to calm your thoughts and enjoy yourself.

Increasing suffering tolerance is an important part of a competitive runner's training. The only way to increase pain tolerance is through familiarization. To resist suffering more successfully, to dig deeper into those reserves, and to perform better in races, you must first break through limits of suffering tolerance in training. Most runners have only physical rationales behind their toughest workouts, but it is important to plan and execute your training with an awareness of the importance of improving suffering tolerance through exposure to suffering. Ironically, suffering in tough workouts is made more tolerable just by embracing the suffering as part of the point. In a 2012 study at the University of Turin, subjects' bodies released more pain-killing substances when the subjects were told the painful exercise they were doing would be beneficial. Italian researchers induced ischemic arm pain in a group of healthy volunteers (they caused blood flow to the subjects' arms to decrease). The subjects were asked to tolerate the subsequent pain for as long as possible. Some of the subjects were told the truth that inducing ischemia in one's arm isn't a good thing. The rest were told the lie that the ischemia would lead to beneficial muscular changes, thus emphasizing the usefulness of the painful endurance task. The researchers found that the group who thought the pain was good for them lasted significantly longer than the first group. Why? "When the meaning of the pain experience is changed from negative to positive through verbal suggestions, the opioid and cannabinoid systems are co-activated and these, in turn, increase pain tolerance," the researchers wrote. In other words, because the subjects believed that the pain was for a good purpose, their bodies released more of the chemicals that help with tolerating pain. This finding goes beyond mere discussions of "mind over matter;" it shows your body can produce documentable physiological changes based on what you believe about a given potentially painful task. The Turin study suggests that your tolerance for ambitious training should increase if you tell yourself there's a point to your pain. You should train your pain threshold as you train your lactic threshold. In fact, the same kinds of intervals that increase your lactic threshold also improve your pain tolerance, because they teach your brain what it feels like to approach your limit and keep going. This is both a physical and psychological process—your body adapts to the exercise, while your mind learns to cope with the discomfort and develops confidence that you can handle the pain. Runners who do interval training decrease their times more quickly than physiological adaptations can take place, showing that psychological adaptations are also taking place. When you hammer yourself in interval sessions, you teach your brain that you can handle the pain. Ignoring fatigue and pain is not a good, long-term competitive strategy. It is better to attend to the messages from your muscles and calibrate training accordingly. Find the state that allows you to run near and occasionally just beyond the boundary between fatigue and pain, a line that is different for each of us and that varies from day to day.

Most runners use a combination of associative (internal) and dissociative (distraction or external) thoughts to tolerate pain. However, distractions such as checking out the scenery or singing to oneself are used less frequently and usually in the early to middle sections of a race. Dissociative techniques seem handiest for maintaining a pace or for finishing a race that is not going well. (Japanese marathoner Sachiko Yamashita says she thinks of music or what she will eat after the race if she is off her pace, subjects that never cross her mind if she is running well.) When the going gets tough, say in the last 10K of a marathon, the tough invariably turn inward.

Here are some real-time strategies to cope with fatigue:

Yield to your fatigue; fighting or becoming angry at fatigue causes tension, frustrates or distracts you, and makes you lose confidence, enthusiasm, and courage--all of which further fatigue. When you feel too fatigued, first slow down slightly and focus on relaxing the body. Then focus on slowing your breathing while maintaining a competitive stride. Many times you will discover that very slight changes in pace can yield large improvements in perceived effort. This is known as association, the act of concentrating intensely on the very act of running. In studies of college runners, John S. Raglin, a sports psychologist at Indiana University, found that less accomplished athletes tended to dissociate, to think of something other than their running to distract themselves. "Sometimes dissociation allows runners to speed up, because they are not attending to their pain and effort," he said. "But what often happens is that they hit a sort of physiological wall that forces them to slow down, so they end up racing inefficiently in a sort of oscillating pace." But association, Dr. Raglin said, is difficult, which may be why most people don't do it. The mind has a slippery way of trying to cope with the pain of running by simply checking out.

Professional runners Kara Goucher, Hendrick Ramaala, Paul Tergat and Lidia Simon all use mantras. They use such words as "fighting" and "battling" with regard to pain. Romanian Lidia Simon (eighth in the 2008 Olympic marathon in 2:27) repeats "Mama" because her mother made her feel as if she could do anything. Goucher also uses the "Divide and Conquer Strategy": "If I'm struggling, I'll break it down--one more lap, one more mile, increments I know I can do," she said. Visualization (crossing the finish line and running lightly) is a practiced strategy for Yamashita. Other strategies for increasing pain tolerance include goal setting, using a reward system and journaling. Goals and rewards tend to enhance the meaningfulness of a task, further increasing the level of suffering you can endure. If you are offered a significant incentive, for example, money, a medal, or fame, to run a P.R., chances are you'll tolerate a far greater degree of discomfort than if you ran without the incentive or goal. With journaling, you grade your mental toughness during workouts and races in your running journal. The very act of paying attention to your tolerance of suffering, coupled with caring about it, will make you able to bear more suffering.

Keep in mind, though, that enjoyment and suffering are not mutually exclusive. It is possible to enjoy and suffer in exercise simultaneously. In fact, enjoyment of exercise increases the capacity to suffer because it makes the suffering seem worthwhile. Many elite runners say their very best performances seem to transcend pain. "It's a common misconception that peak performance requires you to feel maximum pain and suffering. Top athletes will tell you their peak performance hits a sweet spot. They don't feel pain and suffering as much as the exhilaration of the running experience," said Ric Rojas, a former USATF cross-country national champion. In interviews with runners after an Olympic Marathon, "the words pain and suffering very rarely come up. What comes up is I relaxed, I focused, I stayed calm," Rojas said. Ultimately, recognizing pain and fatigue as a normal part of running helps you realize that while it hurts, it's just temporary and it won't leave any lasting damage.

CHAPTER TWELVE

Training and Racing Strategies

"Running is 80% mental." - *Joan Benoit Samuelson*

"Bid me run, and I will strive with things impossible." - *William Shakespeare*

It is important to plan and execute your training with an awareness of the importance of improving mental toughness through exposure to difficult conditions. Here are some ways to do that:

Train alone. Running alone makes you self-reliant. Doing a few half marathons by yourself will improve your mental toughness.

Do workouts that you hate. Many runners hold themselves back by emphasizing the types of training that they like to do over the types of training that they should do. By forcing yourself to do the types of workouts that you find difficult or tedious, you will gradually gain the confidence that comes with overcoming your weaknesses.

Train in adverse conditions. If you always train in ideal conditions, you miss the opportunity to develop the mental toughness that comes from training in bad weather and darkness. Famed University of Oregon coach Bill Dellinger used to have his runners do hard, callousing workouts at 6 a.m. to help instill in them the mental toughness to race fiercely. Do workouts in the heat and humidity. Most runners begin to slow down at 55 degrees and start suffering at 65 degrees. High humidity is also a major problem because it doesn't allow much perspiration or evaporation and as a result your body heats up. Train your body and mind to adapt to heat stress, and push up your threshold. But keep in mind that running too hard in hot and humid conditions will cause you to hit "the wall" sooner than expected. Trying to maintain a goal pace in heat and humidity is like going out too fast early in a race. Temperatures generally increase hour by hour so adjust your pace for the temperature expected at the end of the race.

Pre-performance

Dealing With Stress: Make the Unfamiliar Familiar

Another factor to deal with is stress. Stress is greatest when you feel as if you can't control the situation that you are in. Control what you can control. Familiarize yourself with the course. Preview the course on the day before the race or during your warmup. Plan out all decisions ahead of time, like what you're going to wear, how many energy gels you will keep in your pocket, and how you are going to get to the starting line. Visualizing your performance on a particular course is a great way to get prepared for it.

Pre-performance Routines

There are three types of runners: those whose performance level is better during training than during competitions (underperformers), those who compete at the same performance level at which they train (performers), and those who perform better when they compete than when they train (overperformers). Underperformers tend to focus more on what they don't have or didn't do during training. Doubting yourself, your training, and your ability to perform once the race starts will channel all of the stress and anxiety you are feeling in a negative direction. There are always more things a runner can do to prepare for a race. But when you are at the starting line is the time to focus on what you bring to the race. Push could-haves and should-haves from your mind, and instead recall training highlights. Remember hard runs that you are proud of, the number of kilometers you covered during training, and all the reasons you belong on the starting line. The adrenaline and excitement of the race environment causes the body to go into fight or flight mode. This can develop into panic mode, in which the runner becomes afraid to compete. A characteristic of panic is freezing--the runner does not do the things she would normally do without even thinking about them. Performance routines can help overcome this race-day anxiety.

Routines are thoughts and behaviors automatically integrated into our day. They are of particular importance in sports. Performance routines help athletes to maintain emotional control, particularly under pressure, and regulate mental and emotional performance before, during and after competition. They involve cognitive and behavioral elements that intentionally help regulate arousal and enhance concentration. The concept of focus styles from Chapter 9 applies here. If you have an internal focus style, the goal in your pre-competitive routine should be to put yourself in a place where there are few external distractions and where you can focus on your pre-competitive preparation. To maintain that narrow focus, you want to go through your pre-competitive routine away from people and activities that could distract you. An external focus style means that you need to keep your focus wide during your preparations so that you keep your mind off the upcoming competition and away from thinking too much. If you have an external focus style, the goal in your pre-competitive routine should be to put yourself in a place in which you're unable to become focused internally and think about the competition. Your pre-competitive routine should be done where there is enough activity to draw your focus away from what's going on inside your head. To widen your focus, you want to go through your pre-competitive routine around people and activities that can draw your focus outward.

    Pre-performance routines take place immediately preceding a run or race. Routines before the race should help keep your thoughts positive. Pre-competitive routines are individual. There is no one ideal routine for everyone. For every great runner, you'll see a different routine, but all have common elements. The first step in designing a pre-competitive routine is to make a list of everything you need to do before a race to be prepared. Some of the common elements you can include are meals, review of race strategy, equipment check, mental preparation, and physical warm-up. Next, specify where each step of your routine can be completed. You should use your knowledge of the race site to decide this. For example, if you like to be alone before a competition, find a quiet place where you can get away from people. Finally, establish a schedule for completing your routine. Some athletes like to get to the race site only a short time before they begin. Others like to arrive hours before. A simple pre-competitive routine might include listening to music or an audio book that can keep your mind busy and deter negative thoughts. When the headphones come off, review your personal highlight reel (see Chapter 10: Visualization). That is, channel your past successes by visually recalling your best race or training performances. Before you go to the starting line, give yourself a pep talk reminding yourself why you are there, "I want to be on the starting line. It's the only place where I can begin the pursuit of my running goals". Create a pre-race routine for yourself and stick to it. Everything you do on race day should feel as comfortable as an old habit.

Race Strategies

Many runners go to the starting line of races without a strategy to follow. Such runners are unlikely to feel confident about their ability to win. Successful racing requires using the best tactics for a given race. And because no two races are ever the same in terms of the competition, the weather, and other factors, you should be aware of different racing strategies including front running, even pacing, surging and kicking.

Front Running

Front running is leading the pack from the early stages of a race. Front runners try to build up a lead and demoralize the competition. The front-runner feeds on the confidence of being the leader. This mental energy and optimism propels the front runner to a hard, fast race. This tactic is like a double-edged sword, however. It can cut your competitors by shaking their confidence and breaking their spirit but it can also cut you if you wield it improperly. You must be supremely fit and confident that you can cover the distance alone. Front runners occasionally win a race but usually they just set up a fast race for the eventual winner. The best runner in my age group in my high school cross country competition was an exception to this norm. He was a front runner. He led races from start to finish. But most front runners become victims of "the wall." They go out at a much faster pace than they can maintain, slow down dramatically in the last third of the race, and are passed by the eventual winner who is running at an even pace. Although front runners don't often win, they consistently finish high in their peer group, and often run faster times when they lead from the start.

Divide and Conquer

"I like to break up a workout into smaller, more manageable chunks. I often tell myself, 'You're on the downhill side' when I get halfway, and this makes the workout seem shorter." – John Naber

When training, breaking a long run into several smaller loops makes a daunting distance more manageable. Instead of focusing on running 15 kilometers, for instance, you can just take it one five-kilometer segment at a time. Looping also allows you to create your own aid station. You can stash water and fuel at a set location that you know you'll hit several times. Loops from your house are especially helpful if the weather changes or you need a pit stop. It's comforting to know that an extra layer and a bathroom are never far away. However, looping again and again with no variety in scenery can be boring. Alternate the direction you run on each loop--it's a small change that can be surprisingly refreshing. Likewise, when racing an effective mental trick is to break a race down into bite-sized and optimistic pieces. For example, in the last kilometer of a 10K, you might say, "only 800 meters left until I start my kick," which sounds better than "one kilometer to go".

Even-Pacing

For endurance races of 3,000 meters and above it is not critical to establish your position at the start. Just the opposite is true: It's important not to go out too fast in races. Every runner has heard this pearl of wisdom. So why do so many runners ignore it? Because, for short races, the penalty--a somewhat slower-than-hoped-for 5K time--is not harsh enough to teach the lesson. Your best races will be done using the most common strategy called even-pacing (even splits)--running at a uniform pace until a point in the race when you feel that you can sustain a kick to the finish. If the course is perfectly flat and there is no wind, you can easily run an even pace throughout. But since most courses have hills and most days have wind, you will have to adjust your effort. Kilometers with hills should be run at the same pace as flat kilometers. You will therefore have to work harder during uphill segments, and resist speeding up during downhill segments to maintain your target pace. The same principle applies to running into the wind. Also keep in mind that the objective for this strategy is not to jog for most of the race and then unleash a mad sprint to the finish. From the start, your pace should feel fast and steady, and when you start your kick you should feel tired but in control. Runners who maintain an even pace usually pass their competitors, rather than get passed, as the race unfolds. Passing boosts confidence, which leads to fast finishes. All distance runners should practice the strategy of even-pacing.

On Passing and Being Passed

Pass people like you expect them to stay passed. When passing a competitor in any race, don't just ease by them, fly by them! Make them think you're running so well that there's no need to try to stay with you. You'll crush their spirit and thereby gain more advantage than just the distance between the two of you. You may even want to sneak up on them by hanging back a few strides to recover before you attack.

Pass wide. Along with passing with authority, take a tip from cyclists. In cycling, when a rider makes a move to break away, she swings wide (often to the other side of the road) as she hits the accelerator. Every runner is taught to latch on when being passed but latching on to someone on the other side of the road is hard to do, and often they don't even give chase. Don't look at them--just go hard and get a gap.

Reacting to being passed: When people are running away from you in a race, they fall into two camps: those who are faster than you, and those who are going too fast. The former are irrelevant. You're not going to catch them, so you might as well run your own race. The others are going to burn out. That means they're also irrelevant--unless you burn out chasing them. The truth is that you never know who is, and who isn't, faster than you until the race is over.

When you're suddenly feeling left behind, worthless, or wondering if it's not your day, resist giving up. Wait and see what happens. Being broken comes from assuming that everyone is in the first group. It means you've predetermined the result, at which point it's probably a self-fulfilling prophecy. Remember the old story of the tortoise and the hare.

The Lasso and The Chase

Two other strategies can be combined with even-pacing: The Lasso and The Chase. In the first you imagine "lassoing" the runner two people in front of you. You then let that runner "pull" you past the person immediately in front of you. Stay focused on the person you "lassoed", noting his outfit, hat, and other characteristics. If you focus on details, you'll occupy the left brain and will suffer less. As soon as you pass the first person, focus on the new target two people away. The Chase tactic is employed when you find yourself alone on the course. Chances are that another runner is not far behind you. Instead of going at your comfortable race pace and being caught, speed up and catch the runner ahead of you. Be the cat, not the mouse.

Surging

One of the most common racing mistakes runners make is slowly letting their pace slip, often without even realizing it. As your legs get tired and your breathing becomes more labored, maintaining your goal race pace gets more difficult. Many runners don't know know how to handle this problem. The solution is to analyze the split times from your previous races and identify where you began to slow. If you have the data from your last three or four races, you can usually find a common point where you started to fade. If you're new to a race distance, a good tip to remember is that the slowing point will most often occur just after halfway, usually between halfway and three quarters into the race. For example, the slowing point in a 5K usually happens at around the 3000-meter mark. Once you've identified your slow spot, plan to throw in a surge at this exact moment as you're developing your next race plan. The surge will get you back on pace and serve as a mental reminder not to let the pace slip. This doesn't necessarily make it any easier to keep pushing the pace, but it does prevent the unintentional pace creep that often occurs. Like anything else on race day, you shouldn't use a new strategy without practicing it in training first. Include a few 60-90-second surges during your next run.

Kicking

Kickers feed off the energy and momentum of the other runners by tucking themselves in the pack in the early stages of the race. They then use their fitness and speed to spring away from competitors in the final stage of the race. Runners who possess a kick are hard to beat. The biggest problem for kickers is staying with the leaders until the finish line is within sight. If the kicker drops too far behind the leaders, he must expend a great amount of energy to catch up.

Kickers should practice starting their kicks from different distances. Runners who lack basic speed might experiment with a long, controlled sprint from 400 to 600 meters out. Runners with good speed might wait until the last 100 to 200 meters to start an explosive sprint. One of my personal highlight reel moments is kicking past a runner in the dying moments of a 5K high school cross country run. I emerged from the woods in 6th place and about 100 meters behind the 5th place runner. I kicked, caught up to him, and blew past him while climbing a hill with about 25 meters to go to finish in the top 5. I was the only senior boys runner from my high school to place in the top 5 so it was satisfying for me and good for my school. Whenever you decide to start your kick, be sure to only kick once. A kick uses intermediate fast-twitch and fast-twitch muscle fibers. Because the majority of these fibers function anaerobically, engaging them can lead to rigor. Kick too early or more than once and it'll be hard to walk, let alone run, to the finish line.

Relax at the Finish

If you've ever watched the last 100 meters of a local 5K race, you've probably seen most runners flying down the last straightaway with their faces clenched, arms flailing and veins popping out of their neck as they strain to extract every ounce of speed from their legs. Compare this to how relaxed elite runners are during the final 100 meters of their race. Straining your face and flailing your arms to gain momentum wastes precious energy and distracts you from moving straight ahead as fast and efficiently as possible. This tactic applies to any point in a race, not just the finish. When you hit a rough spot during a race and need to throw in a surge, keep your face relaxed and your form strong. Don't strain and grit your teeth when running uphill, or windmill your arms in an uncontrolled fashion on the way down. Stay relaxed, focus on your form, and let your speed and power come naturally.

Regardless of which strategy you employ, you'll perform better by using a strategy. Keep in mind that races are not just competitive experiences, but ways to evaluate your running progress. Anticipating a race gives more meaning to your daily runs and keeps you motivated.

Epilogue: The Mental Benefits of Running

"Running allows me to set my mind free. Nothing seems impossible, nothing unattainable." - Kara Goucher

"Everything is clearer, heightened. I might be more addicted to this clarity than I am to running itself." – Kristen Armstrong

This book has focused on teaching you psychological techniques to help you become a better runner. I'll conclude it by reversing the focus, and looking at how running improves your psychology. Running transforms you. It transforms your body, the numbers on your scale, and the feeling you get when you hear the words, "bathing suit." It transforms your mood, your thoughts, and your psyche. I don't think there is even one runner whose mental health has not benefited noticeably from running. All forms of exercise benefit the brain, but research indicates that endurance running produces a greater mental payoff. In addition to improved mood, running has been scientifically proven to provide the following mental benefits.

Relieves Stress and Anxiety

Running increases serotonin levels in the brain, which is very effective for stress relief. Many people take up regular running specifically to tackle day-today stress and anxiety. Running helps relieve anxiety and frustrations and get rid of negative feelings. After a stressful day, a run works to relieve stress almost instantly. Get out into the fresh air, with adrenalin pumping, and soon your troubles are out of mind.

Relieves Depression

Running is just as effective as--and in some instances better--than SSRI (selective serotonin reuptake inhibitor) drugs in treating depression. SSRIs work by keeping neurotransmitters such as serotonin and norepinephrine in the synapses longer, improving mood and outlook. It turns out that exercise does the same thing. In studies, patients who were successfully treated with SSRIs relapsed sooner than those who stayed physically active.

Helps Combat Addiction

Many therapists recommend their patients undertake regular exercise to combat their addictions to drugs and alcohol. There are many success stories of people coming off drugs through running, from tobacco and alcohol to the more serious drugs such as cocaine and heroin. When someone stops taking drugs there's a hole left in his life: running conveniently fills this hole. Running is a healthy addiction.

Reduces Mental Fatigue

Running makes you feel more energetic by

bringing down your mental fatigue levels. At times, mental fatigue, more than its physical counterpart, adversely affects your productivity. To overcome mental fatigue, there is nothing better than running daily.

Increases Pain Tolerance

A 2013 study in Australia showed that getting fit increases pain tolerance. The Australian research measured pain threshold and pain tolerance in a group of non-athletes, and then turned half of them into athletes and remeasured pain threshold and pain tolerance after six weeks of training. In one test, the people who trained increased their pain tolerance by 20%. They found a given sensation as painful as before, but could handle that level of discomfort for significantly longer. The non-athletes were as relatively weak or tough as during the first round of testing. Getting fit can make you tougher, and getting tougher might also help you get that much more fit, the researchers speculated. In their words, "Exercise training may facilitate the development of brain function that increases tolerance of these signals and associated sensations, and this increase in tolerance may contribute to improved endurance performance."

Boosts Confidence

Setting and reaching running goals--even small ones--provides a sense of achievement. This will build self-confidence and enhance self-image which spills over into other areas of life. Achieving running goals helps you to believe that you can overcome other obstacles in your life with the same mental approach you take towards running.

Recently the sportswear company Mizuno commissioned the Kenan-Flagler Business School at the University of North Carolina to come up with answers to the question "What if everybody ran?" Using statistics such as census data to model the effects on a large scale, they came up with the following statistics: If everybody ran, people would smoke up to 48,081,000 fewer cigarettes daily, 20 million more people would become great-grandmothers, people would spend 7 billion more hours outside, and up to $143 billion in health care costs would be saved.

All of these benefits in one simple, cheap exercise that can be done independently almost anywhere in most weather!

I'll close with probably my favorite quote on running by Haruki Murakami:

"I'll be happy if running and I can grow old together."

Afterword

Thank you for buying and reading *The Resilient Runner: Mental Toughness Training for Endurance Runners*. I hope you find the techniques within as useful and effective as I have. As you put this book into practice, if you have a success story that you'd like to share, or spot an error, please send me and e-mail at williamaaronpeters@gmail.com.

Word-of-mouth is crucial for any author to succeed. If you liked the book, please consider leaving a review at Amazon, even if it's only a line or two; it would make a big difference and would be much appreciated.

About the Author

William A. Peters is a Canadian writer living in Seoul, Korea. If you want to get an automatic e-mail when Will's next book is released, please sign up to his new release mailing list at http://www.theamateurathlete.net/newreleasemailingli st. Your e-mail address will never be shared and you can unsubscribe at any time.

Say Hello!

Will talks about running and amateur athletics on his blog, The Amateur Athlete, at http://www.theamateurathlete.net. He would love it if you dropped by. Alternatively, you can follow him on Twitter at http://twitter.com/AmateurAthletic, get in touch on Facebook at http://www.facebook.com/williamaaronpeters, or send him an e-mail at: williamaaronpeters@gmail.com.

Dedication

Dedicated with love and respect to my wife
Kyung-Hee Park.

Acknowledgements

I would like to thank Peter Mills for providing
important feedback on this book.

References

10-Minute Toughness: The Mental Training Program for Winning Before the Game Begins by Jason Selk

Exercise for Mood and Anxiety: Proven Strategies for Overcoming Depression and Enhancing Well-Being by Michael Otto and Jasper A.J. Smits

The Inner Game of Tennis: The Classic Guide to the Mental Side of Peak Performance by W. Timothy Gallwey

Galloway's Book on Running 2nd edition by Jeff Galloway

The Mental Athlete by Kay Porter

RUN: The Mind-Body Method of Running by Feel by Matt Fitzgerald

Running with the Mind of Meditation: Lessons for Training Body and Mind by Sakyong Mipham

Running Within: A Guide to Mastering the Body-Mind-Spirit Connection for Ultimate Training and Racing by Jerry Lynch and Warren Scott

Sport Psychology: Concepts and Applications, 7th edition, by Richard H. Cox

Sport Psychology: From Theory to Practice, 5th edition, by Mark H. Anshel

CPSIA information can be obtained
at www.ICGtesting.com
Printed in the USA
LVHW081826041218
599230LV00027B/981/P

ireland

FODOR'S TRAVEL PUBLICATIONS
NEW YORK • TORONTO • LONDON • SYDNEY • AUCKLAND

WWW.FODORS.COM

Contents

KEY TO SYMBOLS

- Map reference
- Address
- Telephone number
- Opening times
- Admission prices
- Bus number
- Train station/DART station
- Ferry/boat
- Driving directions
- Tourist office
- Tours
- Guidebook
- Restaurant
- Café
- Bar
- Shop
- Toilets
- Number of rooms
- No smoking
- Air conditioning
- Swimming pool
- Gym
- Other useful information
- Shopping
- Entertainment
- Nightlife
- Sports
- Activities
- Health and Beauty
- For Children
- Cross reference
- Walk/drive start point